TABLE OF
Contents

This book is a comprehensive resource for property managers overseeing manufactured housing parks in Nevada, offering practical insights and strategies to ensure effective and efficient park management. The guide is structured into ten detailed chapters, each addressing critical aspects of property management, from legal compliance to community building. This guide equips property managers with the essential knowledge and tools needed to excel in managing manufactured housing parks in Nevada, ensuring both operational success and resident satisfaction.

04 Day-to-Day Operations

Day-to-Day Operations

Covers the daily responsibilities of property managers, including property maintenance, utility management, security measures, and fostering positive relationships with residents to ensure a well-run park.

Covers the daily responsibilities of property managers, including property maintenance, utility management, security measures, and fostering positive relationships with residents to ensure a well-run park.

05 Financial Management

Financial Management

Details the financial aspects of park management, such as budgeting, rent collection, financial reporting, and cost control strategies to maintain the park's financial health.

Details the financial aspects of park management, such as budgeting, rent collection, financial reporting, and cost control strategies to maintain the park's financial health.

06 Managing Staff and Vendors

Managing Staff and Vendors

Explores best practices for hiring, training, and managing staff, as well as building and maintaining relationships with vendors and contractors to ensure smooth operations.

Explores best practices for hiring, training, and managing staff, as well as building and maintaining relationships with vendors and contractors to ensure smooth operations.

07 Legal Issues and Risk Management

Legal Issues and Risk Management

Addresses common legal challenges, procedures for evictions and lease terminations, necessary insurance types, and strategies for risk management and crisis preparedness.

Addresses common legal challenges, procedures for evictions and lease terminations, necessary insurance types, and strategies for risk management and crisis preparedness.

08 Enhancing Community Life

Enhancing Community Life

Focuses on building a strong community through organized activities, providing resident services, effective communication strategies, and methods for addressing and resolving resident concerns.

Focuses on building a strong community through organized activities, providing resident services, effective communication strategies, and methods for addressing and resolving resident concerns.

09 Sustainability and Environmental Practices

Sustainability and Environmental Practices

Discusses the implementation of environmentally friendly practices, strategies for improving energy efficiency, effective waste management, and sustainable landscaping to create a greener park environment.

Discusses the implementation of environmentally friendly practices, strategies for improving energy efficiency, effective waste management, and sustainable landscaping to create a greener park environment.

10 Future Trends and Opportunities

Future Trends and Opportunities

Examines emerging technologies, current and future market trends, strategies for park expansion and growth, and long-term planning to ensure the park's continued success and adaptation to future changes.

Examines emerging technologies, current and future market trends, strategies for park expansion and growth, and long-term planning to ensure the park's continued success and adaptation to future changes.

Chapter 1

INTRODUCTION
to Manufactured Housing Parks

Overview of MFH Parks

Manufactured housing refers to homes that are built off-site in a factory setting, then transported and installed at a permanent location. Unlike traditional site-built homes, manufactured homes are constructed under a federal building code administered by the U.S. Department of Housing and Urban Development (HUB), known as the HUB Code. This code sets standards for the design, construction, strength, durability, transportability, fire resistance, and energy efficiency of manufactured homes. The HUB Code also mandates that manufactured homes be built on a permanent chassis, which differentiates them from modular homes. Manufactured homes come in various sizes and configurations, including single-section, multi-section, and even two-story designs. They offer a range of amenities and can be customized to meet the needs and preferences of the buyer. These homes provide an affordable and flexible housing option for many people, making them a vital part of the housing market.

History & Evolution

The concept of manufactured housing has evolved significantly over the years. The earliest forms of manufactured homes were simple, trailer-like structures used for seasonal or temporary living. However, the industry began to change in the mid-20th century as demand for affordable, permanent housing grew.

In 1976, the implementation of the HUB Code marked a significant milestone, establishing national standards for manufactured homes and improving their safety, quality, and durability.

Since then, advancements in construction technology and materials have further enhanced the quality and appeal of manufactured homes. Today's manufactured homes are nearly indistinguishable from site-built homes in terms of aesthetics and functionality, offering a viable solution for affordable housing.

Importance of MFH

Manufactured housing plays a crucial role in providing affordable housing solutions. These homes are typically less expensive to build and maintain than site-built homes, making them accessible to a broader range of people, including first-time homebuyers, retirees, and those seeking affordable living options. Manufactured housing also supports the concept of sustainable living by utilizing efficient construction processes and materials, reducing waste and energy consumption.

In addition to affordability, manufactured housing communities foster a sense of community among residents. Many parks offer shared amenities such as clubhouses, swimming pools, playgrounds, and green spaces, encouraging social interaction and a communal lifestyle. These communities can be particularly appealing to retirees and young families looking for a supportive and cohesive living environment.

Property Manager's Role

The role of a property manager in a manufactured housing park is multifaceted and critical to the success and smooth operation of the community. Property managers are responsible for overseeing the day-to-day operations of the park, ensuring that the property is well-maintained, and addressing the needs and concerns of residents.

Key responsibilities of a property manager include:

1. Maintenance and Repairs: Ensuring that the park's infrastructure, including roads, utilities, and common areas, is properly maintained and that any necessary repairs are promptly addressed.
2. Rent Collection and Financial Management: Collecting rent from residents, managing the park's budget, and handling financial reporting to ensure the park's financial health.
3. Resident Relations: Building and maintaining positive relationships with residents, addressing their concerns, and fostering a sense of community within the park.
4. Compliance with Regulations: Ensuring that the park complies with all local, state, and federal regulations, including zoning laws, tenant rights, and fair housing laws.
5. Staff and Vendor Management: Hiring, training, and managing park staff, as well as coordinating with vendors and contractors for maintenance and repair services.
6. Safety and Security: Implementing measures to ensure the safety and security of residents, including emergency preparedness and response plans.
7. Community Building: Organizing events and activities to foster a sense of community and enhance the quality of life for residents.

Successful property managers possess a combination of organizational, financial, and interpersonal skills. They must be adept at problem-solving, communication, and conflict resolution, as they frequently interact with residents, staff, vendors, and regulatory agencies. Additionally, staying informed about industry trends, legal requirements, and best practices is essential for effective park management.

◆————————————————◆

Chapter 2

UNDERSTANDING
Nevada's Legal Landscape

Overview

This chapter will provide an overview of the legal landscape that property managers must navigate when managing manufactured housing parks in Nevada. Understanding these regulations and laws is crucial for maintaining compliance, protecting tenant rights, and ensuring the smooth operation of the park. The next chapter will delve into the preparations needed to excel in the role of a property manager, including necessary qualifications, continuing education requirements, and practical advice for job applications and onboarding.

State & Local Regulations

Managing a manufactured housing park in Nevada requires a thorough understanding of state and local regulations that govern these communities. These regulations ensure the safety, habitability, and fair treatment of residents while maintaining the integrity of the park.

Familiarize yourself with local Ordinances

In addition to state regulations, take the time to thoroughly research and understand the local ordinances that apply to the manufactured housing park you manage. Local regulations can vary significantly between counties and municipalities, impacting everything from zoning requirements to property maintenance standards. By familiarizing yourself with these ordinances, you can ensure full compliance and avoid potential legal issues down the road. Consider reaching out to local government offices or consulting with legal experts specializing in real estate law to gain a comprehensive understanding of the regulatory landscape in your area.

Nevada Revised Statutes (NRS)

The NRS contains specific provisions related to manufactured housing, particularly in Chapter 118B, which addresses mobile home parks. This chapter covers various aspects, including landlord and tenant rights and responsibilities, park management requirements, and procedures for handling disputes.

Zoning & Land Use

Zoning laws and land use regulations play a significant role in the operation of manufactured housing parks. These regulations determine where manufactured housing parks can be located, the density of homes within the park, and the types of structures and amenities that can be included.

Nevada Administrative Code (NAC)

The NAC provides additional details and administrative guidelines that support the NRS. It includes specific rules for park operations, maintenance standards, and compliance requirements.

Zoning Classifications

Manufactured housing parks are typically zoned in specific residential or mixed-use categories. Understanding the zoning classification of the park is essential for ensuring compliance with local land use regulations.

Local Ordinances

In addition to state regulations, property managers must also comply with local ordinances that may affect land use, zoning, building codes, and health and safety standards. These ordinances vary by county and municipality, so it is crucial to be familiar with the specific regulations applicable to the park's location.

Permitted Uses

Each zoning classification has a list of permitted uses that define what activities and structures are allowed within the park. This includes the types of manufactured homes, accessory buildings, and communal facilities.

Development Standards

Zoning laws also establish development standards, such as minimum lot sizes, setback requirements, maximum building heights, and parking regulations. Adhering to these standards is crucial for maintaining the park's legal standing and aesthetic appeal.

Conditional Use Permits

In some cases, a manufactured housing park may require a conditional use permit (CUP) to operate. A CUP allows for specific uses that are not typically permitted under the standard zoning classification but can be allowed with certain conditions and approvals from local authorities.

Tenant Rights & Responsibilities

Understanding tenant rights and responsibilities is fundamental to managing a manufactured housing park effectively. The NRS Chapter 118B provides a comprehensive framework for landlord-tenant relationships in mobile home parks.

Lease Agreements

Lease agreements are the cornerstone of the landlord-tenant relationship. They should clearly outline the terms and conditions of tenancy, including rent amounts, payment schedules, security deposits, maintenance responsibilities, and rules and regulations of the park.

Rent Increases

The NRS sets specific guidelines for rent increases, including the frequency and notice requirements. Rent increases must be justified and communicated to tenants in advance, typically with a 90-day notice.

Maintenance & Repairs

Tenants are responsible for maintaining their homes and yards, while the park management is responsible for the common areas and infrastructure. Lease agreements should specify the division of maintenance responsibilities to avoid misunderstandings.

Evictions

Evictions in manufactured housing parks are governed by strict legal procedures to protect tenants' rights. Valid reasons for eviction include non-payment of rent, violation of park rules, and failure to maintain the home or lot. Property managers must follow the legal process, including providing proper notice and obtaining a court order if necessary.

Dispute Resolution

Evictions in manufactured housing parks are governed by strict legal procedures to protect tenants' rights. Valid reasons for eviction include non-payment of rent, violation of park rules, and failure to maintain the home or lot. Property managers must follow the legal process, including providing proper notice and obtaining a court order if necessary.

Fair Housing Laws

Fair housing laws are designed to prevent discrimination in housing and ensure that everyone has equal access to housing opportunities. Property managers must comply with both federal and state fair housing laws.

Federal Fair Housing Act

The Fair Housing Act (FHA) prohibits discrimination based on race, color, national origin, religion, sex, familial status, and disability. This means that property managers cannot refuse to rent, set different terms, or otherwise discriminate against tenants or applicants based on these protected characteristics.

Nevada Fair Housing laws

Nevada's fair housing laws mirror federal protections and may include additional protected classes, such as sexual orientation and gender identity. Understanding and complying with these state-specific protections is essential for legal compliance and fostering an inclusive community.

Reasonable Accomodations

Under the FHA, property managers must provide reasonable accommodations and allow reasonable modifications for tenants with disabilities. This could include allowing service animals, installing ramps, or making other changes to policies or physical structures to ensure accessibility.

Chapter 3

PREPARING
for the Role

Qualifications and Skills

Becoming a successful property manager in the manufactured housing park industry requires a specific set of qualifications and skills. While formal education in real estate or property management can be beneficial, practical experience and certain personal attributes are equally important.

Educational Background

While property managers in Nevada's manufactured housing parks are not required to have a specific license, obtaining a degree or certification in real estate, property management, business administration, or a related field can provide valuable knowledge and skills. Additionally, continuing education courses specific to manufactured housing management can enhance your expertise in this niche area.

Experience

Prior experience in property management, customer service, or a related field is highly beneficial. Experience in managing manufactured housing communities or similar residential properties can provide valuable insights into the unique challenges and responsibilities of the role.

Interpersonal Skills

Effective communication and interpersonal skills are essential for building positive relationships with residents, staff, vendors, and regulatory authorities. Property managers must be approachable, empathetic, and capable of resolving conflicts diplomatically.

Organizational Skills

Managing a manufactured housing park requires strong organizational skills to coordinate maintenance tasks, financial management, tenant communication, and administrative duties efficiently. Property managers must be adept at multitasking and prioritizing tasks to ensure the smooth operation of the park.

Continuing Education Requirements

While property managers in Nevada's manufactured housing parks do not need to be licensed, they are required to complete six hours of continuing education annually, as per the Nevada Revised Statutes (NRS). These continuing education courses are designed to keep property managers up-to-date with industry trends, legal regulations, and best practices in property management.

Topics Covered

Continuing education courses for manufactured housing park managers typically cover a range of relevant topics, including landlord-tenant law, fair housing regulations, property maintenance standards, financial management, and emerging industry trends.

Providers

Several organizations and educational institutions offer continuing education courses tailored to property managers in the manufactured housing industry. These courses may be available online or through in-person seminars and workshops.

Benefits

Continuing education not only fulfills statutory requirements but also provides property managers with valuable knowledge and skills that can enhance their effectiveness in managing manufactured housing parks. Staying informed about changes in regulations, industry standards, and best practices can help property managers mitigate risks, improve tenant satisfaction, and ensure compliance with legal requirements.

Job Application Process

Securing a position as a property manager in a manufactured housing park requires a strategic approach to the job application process. While job requirements may vary depending on the specific park and management company, certain steps can increase your chances of success.

Research

Begin by researching potential job opportunities in manufactured housing parks in your desired area. Explore online job boards, company websites, and industry publications to identify openings and learn more about the companies and parks you're interested in.

Tailor Your Resume

Customize your resume to highlight relevant experience, skills, and qualifications that demonstrate your suitability for the role of a property manager in a manufactured housing park. Emphasize your knowledge of landlord-tenant law, property maintenance, financial management, and customer service.

Prepare for Interviews

Practice answering common interview questions related to property management, customer service, conflict resolution, and regulatory compliance. Be prepared to discuss your experience, skills, and approach to managing manufactured housing parks effectively.

Networking

Utilize professional networking platforms, industry events, and local real estate associations to connect with professionals in the manufactured housing industry. Networking can provide valuable insights, job leads, and opportunities for career advancement.

Onboarding & Initial Training

Once you've secured a position as a property manager in a manufactured housing park, the onboarding and initial training process is crucial for getting up to speed and familiarizing yourself with the park's operations and policies.

Orientation

Participate in an orientation session to learn about the park's history, organizational structure, key stakeholders, and operational procedures. This orientation may be conducted by senior management, human resources personnel, or experienced staff members.

Training Programs

Complete any required training programs or courses provided by the park management company. These training programs may cover topics such as park policies and procedures, tenant relations, maintenance protocols, financial management systems, and safety protocols.

Shadowing

Spend time shadowing experienced property managers or staff members to observe daily operations, interact with residents, and familiarize yourself with the park's facilities and amenities.

Documentation

Review and familiarize yourself with essential documentation, including lease agreements, park rules and regulations, financial records, maintenance logs, and emergency procedures. Understanding these documents is critical for effective park management and compliance with legal requirements.

Introduction to Stakeholders

Meet with key stakeholders, including park owners, residents, staff members, vendors, and regulatory authorities. Building positive relationships with these stakeholders is essential for successful park management and community engagement.

This chapter has provided valuable guidance for aspiring property managers preparing to enter the field of manufactured housing park management in Nevada. By acquiring the necessary qualifications and skills, fulfilling continuing education requirements, navigating the job application process strategically, and successfully completing the onboarding and initial training process, property managers can position themselves for success in this dynamic and rewarding industry.

Chapter 4

OPERATIONS
Day-to-Day

Overview

This chapter has explored the critical aspects of day-to-day operations in managing a manufactured housing park in Nevada. By effectively managing property maintenance, utilities, security, and resident relations, property managers can create a safe, secure, and welcoming environment that enhances the quality of life for residents and ensures the overall success of the park.

Property Maintenance

Effective property maintenance is essential for ensuring the safety, functionality, and aesthetic appeal of a manufactured housing park. Property managers are responsible for overseeing routine maintenance tasks and addressing any issues promptly to maintain the overall quality of the park.

Routine Inspections

Conduct regular inspections of the park's infrastructure, including roads, sidewalks, lighting, landscaping, and communal facilities. Identify any maintenance issues, safety hazards, or areas in need of repair.

Preventive Maintenance

Implement a preventive maintenance schedule to address routine tasks such as landscaping, HVAC system servicing, gutter cleaning, and pest control. Proactive maintenance can help prevent costly repairs and extend the lifespan of park assets.

Emergency Repairs

Respond promptly to emergency maintenance requests, such as broken water lines, electrical outages, or structural damage. Develop an emergency response plan and ensure that staff are trained to handle urgent situations effectively.

Contractor Management

Coordinate with qualified contractors and vendors for specialized maintenance tasks that require professional expertise, such as plumbing repairs, electrical work, or landscaping services. Obtain competitive bids, negotiate contracts, and oversee contractor performance to ensure quality workmanship and adherence to budgetary constraints.

Utilities Management

Managing utilities effectively is crucial for maintaining the comfort and convenience of residents while minimizing operational costs for the park. Property managers must oversee the provision of essential utilities such as water, electricity, natural gas, and sewage services.

Billing and Metering

Implement an accurate billing system for utilities consumption, ensuring that residents are billed promptly and accurately for their usage. Install individual meters for each home to track consumption and allocate costs fairly among residents.

Budgeting

Develop a comprehensive budget for utilities expenses based on historical usage data, projected consumption rates, and anticipated price fluctuations. Monitor utility expenses regularly and adjust budget allocations as needed to maintain financial stability.

Conservation Measures

Implement water and energy conservation measures to reduce utility costs and minimize environmental impact. Encourage residents to adopt water-saving and energy-efficient practices, such as installing low-flow fixtures, LED lighting, and programmable thermostats.

Maintenance and Repairs

Monitor utility infrastructure for signs of wear and deterioration, such as leaking pipes, malfunctioning meters, or outdated equipment. Schedule regular maintenance and repairs to address issues promptly and prevent service disruptions.

Security and Safety

Ensuring the safety and security of residents and park facilities is a top priority for property managers. Implementing effective security measures and emergency preparedness protocols is essential for maintaining a safe and secure living environment.

Physical Security

Assess the park's physical security measures, such as fencing, gates, lighting, and surveillance cameras. Identify potential vulnerabilities and implement upgrades or enhancements to improve security and deter criminal activity.

Security Personnel

Consider hiring security personnel or contracting with a security company to patrol the park and respond to security incidents. Trained security personnel can provide a visible deterrent to crime and provide residents with peace of mind.

Emergency Preparedness

Develop and maintain an emergency preparedness plan that outlines procedures for responding to various emergencies, such as natural disasters, fires, medical emergencies, or criminal incidents. Conduct regular drills and training exercises to ensure that staff and residents are prepared to respond effectively in emergencies.

Community Policing

Develop and maintain an emergency preparedness plan that outlines procedures for responding to various emergencies, such as natural disasters, fires, medical emergencies, or criminal incidents. Conduct regular drills and training exercises to ensure that staff and residents are prepared to respond effectively in emergencies.

Resident Relations

Building positive relationships with residents is essential for fostering a sense of community and ensuring resident satisfaction. Property managers play a critical role in addressing resident concerns, resolving disputes, and promoting a supportive living environment.

Open Communication

Maintain open lines of communication with residents through regular newsletters, community meetings, and electronic communication channels. Encourage residents to voice their concerns, provide feedback, and participate in park activities and events.

Conflict Resolution

Develop effective conflict resolution strategies to address disputes or disagreements between residents, staff, or neighbors. Act as a neutral mediator and work collaboratively with all parties involved to find mutually acceptable solutions.

Tenant Engagement

Engage residents in park decision-making processes by soliciting their input on community issues, park improvements, and policy changes. Empowering residents to participate in decision-making can foster a sense of ownership and pride in the community.

Tenant Education

Provide residents with information and resources to help them understand their rights and responsibilities as park residents. Educate residents about park rules and regulations, lease agreements, maintenance procedures, and emergency protocols to promote compliance and accountability.

Community Watch Program

Empower residents to take an active role in enhancing security within the manufactured housing park by establishing a community watch program. Encourage residents to participate in neighborhood patrols, report suspicious activity promptly, and communicate with park management and local law enforcement as needed. A community watch program not only enhances security but also fosters a sense of community ownership and collaboration in maintaining a safe living environment. Regular meetings, training sessions, and outreach efforts can help residents feel empowered and engaged in creating a secure community for everyone.

Chapter 5

FINANCIAL
Management

This chapter will explore key principles and practices of financial management in managing a manufactured housing park. By developing comprehensive budgets, implementing effective rent collection policies, and maintaining accurate financial records and reporting, property managers can ensure financial stability, transparency, and accountability in park operations.

Budgeting & Financial Planning

Effective financial management is essential for the long-term success and sustainability of a manufactured housing park. Property managers must develop and adhere to a comprehensive budget that accounts for all revenue and expenses associated with park operations.

Revenue Sources

Identify and assess all sources of revenue for the park, including lot rents, utility fees, late fees, pet fees, and income from amenities such as laundry facilities or storage units. Determine the projected income from each revenue source based on historical data and anticipated occupancy rates.

Expense Categories

Categorize expenses into essential operational costs such as utilities, maintenance, repairs, landscaping, insurance, property taxes, and administrative expenses. Allocate funds for capital improvements, reserve funds, and contingency reserves to cover unexpected expenses or emergencies.

Budget Development

Develop an annual budget that balances projected revenues with anticipated expenses while maintaining financial stability and meeting the park's operational needs. Consider factors such as inflation, market trends, regulatory changes, and seasonal fluctuations when projecting income and expenses.

Monitoring & Review

Regularly monitor financial performance against the budget, comparing actual income and expenses to projected amounts. Conduct periodic budget reviews to identify variances, adjust forecasts as needed, and reallocate resources to align with strategic priorities and financial objectives.

Rent Collection & Pricing

Rent collection is a critical aspect of financial management in a manufactured housing park. Property managers must establish clear rent collection policies, communicate expectations to residents, and ensure timely payment to maintain cash flow and meet financial obligations.

Rent Setting

Determine appropriate rent levels based on market conditions, comparable rents in the area, amenities offered, and the quality of the park facilities. Consider factors such as demand, occupancy rates, and tenant preferences when setting rent prices to maximize revenue while remaining competitive in the market.

Rent Increase Policies

Establish transparent policies for rent increases, including frequency, notice periods, and criteria for determining the amount of rent adjustments. Comply with state and local regulations governing rent increases and provide residents with sufficient notice of any changes to rental rates.

Payment Methods

Offer multiple payment options to residents, including online payments, automatic bank transfers, credit card payments, and traditional methods such as check or money order. Make it easy and convenient for residents to pay rent on time to minimize delinquencies and late fees.

Collections Process

Implement a systematic collections process to address delinquent accounts promptly and effectively. Follow established procedures for notifying residents of overdue payments, imposing late fees, and pursuing legal action if necessary to recover unpaid rent.

Financial Reporting

Accurate and timely financial reporting is essential for monitoring the park's financial performance, tracking expenses, and making informed business decisions. Property managers must maintain detailed records and prepare financial reports that provide transparency and accountability to park owners, investors, and regulatory authorities.

Income Statements

Prepare monthly, quarterly, and annual income statements that summarize the park's revenue, expenses, and net income. Include line items for each revenue source and expense category to provide a comprehensive overview of financial performance.

Balance Sheets

Maintain balance sheets that document the park's assets, liabilities, and equity position. Include details such as cash reserves, accounts receivable, property values, outstanding debts, and owner equity to assess the park's financial health and solvency.

Cash Flow Statements

Generate cash flow statements that track the park's incoming and outgoing cash flows over a specified period. Identify sources of cash inflows and outflows, including operating activities, investing activities, and financing activities, to evaluate liquidity and cash management strategies.

Budget Variance Analysis

Conduct variance analysis to compare actual financial results to budgeted amounts and identify discrepancies or deviations. Analyze the reasons for budget variances and take corrective actions to address deficiencies, improve financial performance, and optimize resource allocation.

Chapter 6

MANAGING
Staff & Vendors

This chapter will explore the importance of effective staff and vendor management in the successful operation of a manufactured housing park. By recruiting and hiring qualified staff, providing ongoing training and development opportunities, and establishing strong relationships with reliable vendors, property managers can ensure efficient park operations and deliver high-quality services to residents.

Recruitment & Hiring

Building a competent and reliable team is crucial for the successful operation of a manufactured housing park. Property managers must develop effective recruitment strategies, attract qualified candidates, and implement a thorough hiring process to select the best candidates for staff positions.

Job Descriptions

Develop detailed job descriptions outlining the roles, responsibilities, qualifications, and expectations for each staff position within the park. Clearly define the skills, experience, and attributes required for success in each role to attract suitable candidates.

Recruitment Channels

Utilize a variety of recruitment channels to reach potential candidates, including online job boards, industry associations, local newspapers, social media platforms, and professional networking events. Leverage employee referrals and word-of-mouth recommendations to identify qualified candidates.

Screening & Selection

Establish a structured screening and selection process to evaluate candidates' qualifications, experience, and fit with the park's culture and values. Conduct initial phone screenings, interviews, and reference checks to assess candidates' suitability for the position.

Training & Onboarding

Provide comprehensive training and onboarding for newly hired staff members to familiarize them with park policies, procedures, and expectations. Develop training programs that cover essential topics such as customer service, safety protocols, maintenance procedures, and emergency response protocols.

Staff Development & Training

Investing in staff development and training is essential for enhancing employee skills, knowledge, and performance. Property managers should provide ongoing training and professional development opportunities to help staff members excel in their roles and contribute to the park's success.

Screening & Selection

Encourage staff members to pursue continuing education opportunities, certifications, and professional development courses relevant to their roles. Provide financial support, resources, and incentives to support employees' ongoing learning and skill development.

Cross-Training

Cross-train staff members to perform multiple roles and responsibilities within the park. Develop a versatile workforce capable of filling in for absent employees, addressing staffing shortages, and adapting to changing operational needs.

Performance Feedback

Provide regular feedback and performance evaluations to staff members to recognize achievements, address areas for improvement, and set performance goals. Establish a culture of open communication and constructive feedback to promote continuous learning and growth.

Team Building

Foster a positive and collaborative work environment through team-building activities, group outings, and recognition programs. Encourage teamwork, cooperation, and mutual support among staff members to enhance morale and productivity.

Vendor Management

Effective vendor management is essential for ensuring timely and cost-effective maintenance and repair services within the manufactured housing park. Property managers must establish strong relationships with vendors, negotiate favorable contracts, and monitor vendor performance to maintain high standards of service delivery.

Vendor Selection

Evaluate potential vendors based on factors such as reputation, experience, pricing, quality of work, and responsiveness to inquiries. Obtain multiple quotes and conduct thorough due diligence to select vendors that align with the park's needs and standards.

Contract Negotiation

Negotiate contracts with vendors that clearly define the scope of work, pricing structure, service level agreements, and performance metrics. Ensure that contracts include provisions for quality assurance, dispute resolution, and termination clauses to protect the park's interests.

Monitoring & Oversight

Monitor vendor performance regularly to ensure compliance with contractual obligations, quality standards, and deadlines. Conduct site inspections, review workmanship, and solicit feedback from residents to assess vendor performance and address any issues or concerns promptly.

Relationship Building

Cultivate positive and collaborative relationships with vendors based on mutual respect, trust, and professionalism. Communicate openly, provide clear expectations, and resolve conflicts or disputes in a fair and timely manner to maintain strong vendor partnerships.

Chapter 7

LEGAL & RISK
Issues *Management*

This chapter has addressed the legal obligations, risk management strategies, and dispute resolution techniques relevant to managing a manufactured housing park in Nevada. By understanding legal requirements, implementing risk mitigation measures, and seeking legal advice when needed, property managers can protect the park's interests and ensure compliance with applicable laws and regulations.

Understanding Legal Obligations

Property managers in manufactured housing parks must navigate a complex legal landscape to ensure compliance with state, federal, and local regulations. Understanding key legal obligations and staying abreast of legal developments is essential for mitigating risks and avoiding legal liabilities.

Landlord-Tenant Law

Familiarize yourself with Nevada's landlord-tenant laws, including provisions specific to manufactured housing parks outlined in the Nevada Revised Statutes (NRS) Chapter 118B. Understand tenant rights, eviction procedures, lease requirements, and landlord obligations to ensure compliance and protect resident rights.

Fair Housing Laws

Adhere to federal and state fair housing laws that prohibit discrimination based on race, color, religion, national origin, sex, familial status, disability, and other protected characteristics. Implement policies and practices that promote fair housing and ensure equal treatment of all residents.

Zoning & Land Use Regulations

Comply with local zoning and land use regulations governing manufactured housing parks, including requirements related to park development, occupancy limits, setback requirements, and permitted land uses. Obtain necessary permits and approvals for park expansions, renovations, or other modifications to avoid legal violations.

Contract Law

Understand the principles of contract law and ensure that all contracts and agreements entered into on behalf of the park are legally enforceable and binding. Review contracts carefully, seek legal advice if necessary, and negotiate favorable terms to protect the park's interests.

Risk Assessment & Litigation

Identifying and mitigating potential risks is essential for protecting the manufactured housing park from financial losses, legal disputes, and safety hazards. Property managers should conduct regular risk assessments, implement risk management strategies, and maintain appropriate insurance coverage to safeguard the park's assets and residents.

Property Inspections

Conduct regular inspections of park facilities, infrastructure, and common areas to identify potential safety hazards, maintenance issues, and compliance deficiencies. Address any hazards or deficiencies promptly to minimize the risk of accidents or injuries.

Liability Insurance

Obtain comprehensive liability insurance coverage to protect the park against claims of property damage, bodily injury, or negligence. Review insurance policies regularly, ensure adequate coverage limits, and consider additional coverage options such as umbrella policies or professional liability insurance.

Emergency Preparedness

Develop and implement emergency preparedness plans that outline procedures for responding to natural disasters, fires, medical emergencies, or other crisis situations. Conduct regular drills, train staff on emergency protocols, and maintain emergency supplies and equipment to ensure readiness.

Legal Compliance Audits

Conduct periodic audits of park operations, policies, and procedures to assess compliance with applicable laws, regulations, and industry standards. Address any compliance deficiencies identified during audits and take corrective action to mitigate legal risks.

Dispute Resolution & Legal Representation

Despite proactive risk management efforts, disputes may arise that require legal intervention or resolution. Property managers should be prepared to handle disputes effectively, seek legal advice when necessary, and engage legal representation to protect the park's interests and rights.

Mediation & Arbitration

Attempt to resolve disputes through negotiation, mediation, or arbitration before resorting to litigation. Mediation and arbitration can be cost-effective and less adversarial than traditional court proceedings, allowing parties to reach mutually satisfactory resolutions.

Legal Consultation

Consult with legal professionals specializing in real estate law, landlord-tenant law, or manufactured housing regulations to obtain guidance on complex legal issues or disputes. Seek legal advice early in the dispute resolution process to understand rights, obligations, and potential legal strategies.

Litigation Management

Engage legal representation to defend the park's interests in litigation or legal proceedings, such as eviction cases, contract disputes, or regulatory enforcement actions. Work closely with legal counsel to prepare legal arguments, gather evidence, and present a strong defense in court.

Record Keeping

Maintain detailed records of all communications, transactions, and interactions related to legal matters or disputes. Documenting conversations, agreements, and decisions can provide valuable evidence and support legal defenses in case of litigation or regulatory inquiries.

Document Everything

In matters of legal compliance and risk management, thorough documentation is your best defense. Keep detailed records of all communications, transactions, inspections, and legal matters related to the management of the manufactured housing park. Clear documentation not only helps you stay organized but also provides valuable evidence and support in the event of disputes, litigation, or regulatory inquiries.

In addition to serving as evidence of compliance, risk mitigation, and dispute resolution, thorough documentation also fosters transparency and accountability in park management. By maintaining detailed records of all relevant activities and interactions, property managers demonstrate a commitment to open communication and responsible stewardship of the park's resources. Transparent documentation allows residents, stakeholders, and regulatory authorities to review the park's operations and decisions, fostering trust and confidence in the management team. Moreover, clear documentation promotes consistency and continuity in park management, ensuring that essential information is preserved and accessible even in the event of staff turnover or transitions. Ultimately, by documenting everything comprehensively, property managers not only protect themselves legally but also uphold the integrity and professionalism of the manufactured housing park.

Chapter 8

ENHANCING
Community Life

This chapter will explore various strategies for enhancing community life in a manufactured housing park. By organizing community-building activities, providing essential resident services and support, implementing effective communication strategies, and addressing resident concerns promptly, property managers can create a thriving, cohesive, and supportive community. Enhancing community life not only improves resident satisfaction but also contributes to the long-term success and stability of the park.

Community Building Activities

Creating a vibrant community life within a manufactured housing park involves organizing various events and activities that bring residents together. These activities help build relationships, foster a sense of belonging, and enhance the overall living experience.

Organizing Events

Regularly schedule community events such as holiday celebrations, barbecues, movie nights, and potlucks. These gatherings provide residents with opportunities to socialize and get to know their neighbors. Consider incorporating themed events that cater to different interests and cultural backgrounds to ensure inclusivity and diversity.

Interest Groups & Clubs

Encourage the formation of interest-based groups and clubs within the community. Book clubs, gardening groups, fitness classes, and hobby workshops can provide residents with common interests a platform to connect and engage. Supporting these groups with meeting spaces and resources can enhance their effectiveness and participation.

Youth & Family Activities

Organize activities specifically designed for families and children, such as game nights, sports leagues, and arts and crafts sessions. Creating a family-friendly environment helps build a cohesive community and ensures that all age groups have opportunities to participate and enjoy.

Resident Services & Support

Providing a range of services and support to residents is essential for enhancing community life and ensuring resident satisfaction. These services can address various needs and contribute to a higher quality of living within the park.

On-Site Services

Offer convenient on-site services such as laundry facilities, fitness centers, and community rooms. These amenities enhance the living experience and provide residents with valuable resources within easy reach.

Resident Meetings

Consider incorporating themed resident meetings, such as "Safety and Security Night" or "Community Improvement Workshop," to focus on specific topics of interest and engage residents more deeply. Additionally, offer virtual meeting options for those unable to attend in person, ensuring all residents have the opportunity to participate and stay informed.

Resident Assistance Programs

Develop programs to assist residents with specific needs, such as financial counseling, healthcare referrals, and job placement services. Collaborate with local organizations and service providers to offer these programs and ensure residents have access to essential support.

Maintenance & Upkeep

Ensure that maintenance services are prompt and efficient. Regularly scheduled maintenance checks and a responsive repair system can greatly improve residents' comfort and satisfaction. Providing a clear process for residents to report maintenance issues and receive updates on repairs is also crucial.

Communication Strategies

Effective communication is key to building trust and maintaining a positive relationship with residents. Property managers must establish clear and consistent communication channels to keep residents informed and engaged.

Newsletters & Bulletins

Distribute regular newsletters or bulletins that include updates on park activities, upcoming events, maintenance schedules, and important announcements. Both digital and print formats can be used to accommodate all residents.

Digital Communication

Utilize digital communication platforms such as email, social media groups, and community apps to provide real-time updates and facilitate two-way communication. Digital platforms allow for instant communication and can be more accessible for many residents.

Notice Boards & Flyers

Place notice boards in common areas and distribute flyers to inform residents about events, policy changes, and other important information. Visual reminders in high-traffic areas can ensure that all residents are kept in the loop.

Addressing Resident Concerns

Addressing and resolving resident concerns promptly and effectively is crucial for maintaining a positive community atmosphere. Property managers should have clear procedures in place for handling complaints and ensuring residents feel heard and valued.

Open Door Policy

Implement an open door policy that encourages residents to share their concerns directly with management. Being approachable and available can help resolve issues before they escalate and shows residents that their input is valued.

Complaint Resolution Process

Establish a formal process for residents to submit complaints and receive timely responses. Ensure that all complaints are documented, investigated, and addressed fairly. Communicating the steps being taken to resolve an issue and providing regular updates can help build trust.

Conflict Mediation

When conflicts arise between residents, offer mediation services to facilitate a resolution. Acting as a neutral party, the property manager can help mediate discussions and find mutually acceptable solutions. Training staff in conflict resolution techniques can enhance their effectiveness in these situations.

Chapter 9

PRACTICES
Sustainability & Environmental

This chapter will cover the essential aspects of sustainability and environmental practices for a manufactured housing park. By implementing green practices, improving energy efficiency, adopting effective waste management strategies, and creating sustainable landscapes, property managers can significantly enhance the park's environmental footprint. These efforts not only contribute to a healthier planet but also create a more attractive and cost-effective living environment for residents.

Green Practices

Implementing environmentally friendly practices in your manufactured housing park not only helps the environment but also can reduce costs and enhance the park's appeal to eco-conscious residents. Integrating green practices into the daily operations and infrastructure of the park demonstrates a commitment to sustainability and can improve the quality of life for residents.

Recycling Program

Establish a comprehensive recycling program that encourages residents to recycle paper, plastic, glass, and metal. Provide clearly labeled recycling bins throughout the park and educate residents on what materials can be recycled. Partnering with local recycling services can ensure that collected materials are properly processed.

Water Conservation

Implement water-saving measures such as low-flow faucets, showerheads, and toilets. Encourage residents to conserve water by providing tips on water-saving practices, such as fixing leaks promptly and using drought-resistant plants in landscaping. Installing rainwater harvesting systems can also reduce water usage and provide an eco-friendly water source for irrigation.

Green Cleaning Products

Use environmentally friendly cleaning products for maintaining common areas and facilities. Green cleaning products reduce the release of harmful chemicals into the environment and can improve indoor air quality. Encourage residents to use these products in their homes as well.

Energy Efficiency

Improving energy efficiency in the park can significantly reduce energy consumption and costs. Energy-efficient practices not only benefit the environment but also contribute to a more sustainable and cost-effective operation.

Energy-Efficient Lighting

Replace traditional incandescent bulbs with energy-efficient LED or CFL bulbs in common areas and outdoor lighting fixtures. These bulbs use less energy, have a longer lifespan, and provide substantial cost savings over time.

Energy Audits

Conduct regular energy audits to identify areas where energy is being wasted and where improvements can be made. Audits can reveal inefficiencies in heating, cooling, and electrical systems, allowing for targeted upgrades and optimizations.

Solar Energy

Consider installing solar panels to generate renewable energy for the park. Solar energy can reduce reliance on grid electricity, lower energy costs, and decrease the park's carbon footprint. Explore incentives and rebates available for solar installations to offset initial costs.

Insulation & Weatherization

Improve the insulation and weatherization of park buildings to reduce energy loss. Proper insulation, weatherstripping, and sealing of windows and doors can enhance heating and cooling efficiency, leading to energy savings and increased comfort for residents.

Waste Management

Improve the insulation and weatherization of park buildings to reduce energy loss. Proper insulation, weatherstripping, and sealing of windows and doors can enhance heating and cooling efficiency, leading to energy savings and increased comfort for residents.

Composting

Encourage residents to compost organic waste such as food scraps and yard trimmings. Provide information on how to start a composting program and the benefits of composting. Designate a communal composting area and offer workshops on composting techniques.

Waste Reduction

Implement waste reduction strategies by promoting the use of reusable items over disposable ones. Encourage residents to use reusable bags, containers, and water bottles. Organize community swap events where residents can exchange unwanted items instead of discarding them.

Proper Disposal

Ensure that hazardous materials such as batteries, electronics, and chemicals are disposed of properly. Provide information on local hazardous waste disposal sites and organize periodic collection events to facilitate safe disposal.

Litter Prevention

Maintain clean common areas by placing adequate trash receptacles throughout the park and organizing regular clean-up events. Educate residents on the importance of keeping the community clean and litter-free.

Sustainable Landscaping

Creating and maintaining sustainable landscapes enhances the beauty of the park while conserving resources and supporting the local ecosystem. Sustainable landscaping practices can also reduce maintenance costs and promote environmental stewardship.

Native Plants

Use native plants in landscaping as they are well-adapted to the local climate and require less water, fertilizer, and maintenance. Native plants also provide habitat and food for local wildlife, promoting biodiversity.

Xeriscaping

Implement xeriscaping techniques to create attractive, low-water-use landscapes. Xeriscaping involves using drought-tolerant plants, efficient irrigation systems, and mulching to conserve water. This approach reduces the need for supplemental watering and minimizes water consumption.

Organic Landscaping

Practice organic landscaping by avoiding synthetic fertilizers and pesticides. Use natural fertilizers, such as compost and mulch, and implement integrated pest management (IPM) techniques to control pests. Organic landscaping promotes soil health and reduces environmental pollution.

Water-Efficient Irrigation

Install water-efficient irrigation systems, such as drip irrigation or smart sprinkler systems, to reduce water waste. These systems deliver water directly to the root zones of plants, minimizing evaporation and runoff. Schedule irrigation during early morning or late evening hours to further conserve water.

Active Listening is Key

When addressing resident complaints or concerns, practice active listening by giving your full attention, acknowledging their feelings, and repeating back what you've heard to ensure understanding. This approach not only helps in resolving issues effectively but also builds trust and demonstrates that you value their input.

Active listening is a powerful tool for property managers in maintaining positive resident relations. When a resident voices a complaint or concern, it's crucial to give them your undivided attention. This means minimizing distractions, making eye contact, and nodding or using verbal affirmations to show you are engaged. By focusing entirely on the resident's words and emotions, you convey respect and empathy, which can help de-escalate tensions and foster a cooperative atmosphere. Repeating back or summarizing what the resident has said also ensures clarity and demonstrates that you have genuinely understood their perspective, further building trust.

Moreover, active listening not only helps in resolving individual issues but also contributes to a broader culture of transparency and responsiveness within the community. When residents feel heard and understood, they are more likely to communicate openly and honestly, providing valuable feedback that can guide improvements in park management. This proactive engagement can prevent minor issues from becoming major conflicts, enhance resident satisfaction, and promote a harmonious living environment. Encouraging staff to adopt active listening techniques in all interactions can lead to stronger, more positive relationships with residents, ultimately contributing to the park's overall success and stability.

Chapter 10

FUTURE TRENDS
&Opportunities

This chapter will explore the future trends and opportunities in the manufactured housing industry. By embracing technological advances, staying informed about market trends, strategically planning for expansion and growth, and developing long-term plans, property managers can ensure the continued success and sustainability of their parks. Preparing for the future and adapting to changes will help create thriving communities that meet the evolving needs of residents.

Technological Advances

The manufactured housing industry is continually evolving, with technological advances offering new opportunities for park management and resident satisfaction. Staying informed about these innovations can help property managers stay ahead of the curve and enhance their operations.

Smart Home Technology

The integration of smart home technology in manufactured homes is becoming increasingly popular. Features like smart thermostats, lighting, and security systems can enhance the convenience and efficiency of homes. Property managers can consider promoting these technologies to residents and exploring partnerships with providers to offer installation services.

Property Management Software

Advanced property management software can streamline operations and improve efficiency. These platforms offer tools for rent collection, maintenance requests, communication, and financial reporting. Investing in robust property management software can save time, reduce errors, and improve resident satisfaction.

Renewable Energy Solutions

Emerging renewable energy technologies, such as advanced solar panels and wind turbines, provide opportunities for parks to become more energy-independent and sustainable. Implementing these solutions can reduce energy costs and attract eco-conscious residents.

Virtual Tours & Online Leasing

Virtual tours and online leasing platforms are becoming standard in the housing market. These technologies allow prospective residents to view and lease homes remotely, expanding the potential market and making the leasing process more convenient and efficient.

Market Trends

Understanding current and future trends in the manufactured housing market is crucial for making informed decisions and staying competitive. Property managers should stay updated on these trends to anticipate changes and capitalize on new opportunities.

Affordable Housing Demand

The demand for affordable housing continues to grow, making manufactured housing an attractive option for many. Property managers should highlight the affordability and benefits of manufactured homes in their marketing strategies to attract cost-conscious residents.

Aging Population

As the population ages, there is an increasing need for senior-friendly housing options. Manufactured housing parks can cater to this demographic by offering amenities and services tailored to seniors, such as accessibility features, healthcare partnerships, and social activities.

Urbanization & Space Constraints

With urban areas facing space constraints and high housing costs, manufactured housing parks in suburban or rural areas are becoming more appealing. Property managers can market their parks as affordable and spacious alternatives to urban living, emphasizing the community and lifestyle benefits.

Sustainability Focus

Environmental sustainability is becoming a key consideration for many consumers. Emphasizing green practices, energy efficiency, and sustainable living options can attract environmentally conscious residents and set the park apart from competitors.

Expansion & Growth

Strategically planning for expansion and growth is essential for the long-term success of a manufactured housing park. Property managers should consider various strategies to expand their operations and increase their market share.

Acquiring Additional Land

Acquiring adjacent land for expansion can provide opportunities to add more homes and amenities. Conducting thorough market research and feasibility studies is crucial to ensure that expansion efforts align with demand and financial viability.

Developing New Amenities

Investing in new amenities can attract more residents and enhance the park's appeal. Consider adding facilities such as swimming pools, fitness centers, community centers, and recreational areas. Upgrading existing amenities can also improve resident satisfaction and retention.

Marketing & Outreach

Expanding marketing efforts to reach a broader audience can drive growth. Utilize digital marketing, social media, and community partnerships to promote the park. Highlight unique selling points, such as affordability, community atmosphere, and green practices, to differentiate the park from competitors.

Diversifying Resident Demographics

Attracting a diverse range of residents, including families, young professionals, and retirees, can create a vibrant and balanced community. Offering various home styles, sizes, and price points can appeal to different demographic groups and increase occupancy rates.

Long-Term Planning

Long-term planning is critical for ensuring the continued success and stability of a manufactured housing park. Property managers should develop comprehensive plans that address future challenges and opportunities.

Financial Planning

Implementing sound financial planning practices is essential for long-term success. Develop detailed budgets, forecast future expenses and revenues, and create contingency plans for economic downturns. Regularly review financial performance and adjust strategies as needed.

Infrastructure Upgrades

Investing in infrastructure upgrades can improve the park's longevity and functionality. Regularly assess the condition of roads, utilities, and common areas, and plan for necessary repairs and enhancements. Upgrading infrastructure can also increase property values and resident satisfaction.

Regulatory Compliance

Staying informed about regulatory changes and ensuring compliance is crucial for avoiding legal issues and penalties. Monitor local, state, and federal regulations affecting manufactured housing parks and adjust policies and practices accordingly.

Resident Engagement

Maintaining strong resident engagement and satisfaction is vital for long-term stability. Continuously seek feedback, address concerns, and foster a sense of community. Happy residents are more likely to stay long-term and recommend the park to others.

Strategic Partnerships

Building strategic partnerships with local businesses, service providers, and community organizations can provide additional resources and support. Collaborations can enhance the park's amenities, services, and overall appeal.

"... seek feedback, address concerns..."

 **KAYLAFENNER**

THANK
You

Thank you for embarking on this journey to enhance your skills and knowledge in managing manufactured housing parks. Your dedication to creating thriving, sustainable, and vibrant communities is commendable. I hope this book has provided you with valuable insights, practical strategies, and inspiration to elevate your park management practices. As you implement these ideas and continue to grow, remember that your efforts contribute to the well-being and happiness of countless residents. Your commitment to excellence and continuous improvement is what makes a significant difference. Thank you for making our communities better, one step at a time.